MARKS &
SPENCER

soups

simple and delicious easy-to-make recipes

Frances Ros

Marks and Spencer p.l.c.
Baker Street, London, W1U 8EP

www.marksandspencer.com

Copyright © Exclusive Editions 2002

Titles in this series are subject to availability.

ISBN: 1-84273-846-1

Printed in China

Produced by the Bridgewater Book Company Ltd.

Photographer Calvey Taylor-Haw

Home Economist Ruth Pollock

The crockery featured on the following pages can be
purchased at Marks and Spencer's stores:

page 24 – white bowl & plate,
     02733/4285 & 02733/4280

page 80 – silver-rimmed bowl & plate,
     02148/5306 & 02148/5302

page 94 – white and dark blue bowl & plate,
     02733/1002 & 02733/1005

NOTES FOR THE READER

- This book uses both metric and imperial measurements. Follow the same units of measurement throughout; do not mix metric and imperial.

- All spoon measurements are level: teaspoons are assumed to be 5 ml, and tablespoons are assumed to be 15 ml.

- Unless otherwise stated, milk is assumed to be full fat, eggs and individual vegetables such as potatoes are medium, and pepper is freshly ground black pepper.

- Recipes using raw or very lightly cooked eggs should be avoided by infants, the elderly, pregnant women, convalescents, and anyone suffering from an illness.

- The times given are an approximate guide only. Preparation times differ according to the techniques used by different people and the cooking times may also vary from those given. Optional ingredients, variations or serving suggestions have not been included in the calculations.

contents

introduction

There is no substitute for good, home-made soup, and creating soups at home can be tremendously enjoyable. You need little in the way of basic equipment, just a large saucepan with a lid and a sharp knife for chopping. A large frying pan or wok is also helpful, but not essential.

Soup can be very economical to make – you can use leftovers to make some delicious concoctions, from light starters and snacks to more substantial soups that are meals in themselves. On special occasions, you can splash out on more expensive ingredients and create impressive soups that will grace any dinner table.

Soups are very nutritious, too, and can be packed with healthy ingredients such as vegetables, fish, pulses and rice. Many are low in fat, and high-fat ingredients such as cream can be replaced with lower fat alternatives.

Soup is also a popular international food. Many of the recipes included in this book reflect the rich diversity of the different cuisines found across the world, so wherever you happen to be – and whatever the occasion – you are bound to find something in its pages to satisfy your taste and delight your dinner guests.

guide to recipe key		
	very easy	Recipes are graded as follows: 1 pea = easy; 2 peas = very easy; 3 peas = extremely easy.
	serves 4	Recipes generally serve four people. Simply halve the ingredients to serve two, taking care not to mix metric and imperial measurements.
	10 minutes	Preparation time. Where marinating, chilling or cooling are involved, these times have been added on separately: eg, 15 minutes + 30 minutes to marinate.
	10 minutes	Cooking time. Cooking times do not include the cooking of side dishes or accompaniments served with the main dishes.

mushroom & sherry soup
page 18

bouillabaisse
page 42

sausage & red cabbage soup
page 70

spicy lentil soup
page 76

vegetable soups

Vegetables are very healthy foods and make nutritious, satisfying ingredients in soups. The combinations of texture and flavour in this section are endless. From the chilled Gazpacho, with its ripe tomatoes and red peppers, to the delightful Vegetable Soup with Pesto, packed with fresh basil and garlic, there are mouthwatering recipes for every season using every type of vegetable. Alcohol is also a great favourite in soups, so why not try the Mushroom & Sherry Soup? And for cheese lovers, the Sweet Potato & Stilton Soup is an absolute must.

gazpacho

		ingredients	
extremely easy		500 g/1 lb 2 oz large ripe tomatoes	GARNISH
		4 tbsp extra-virgin olive oil	croûtons (see page 24)
serves 4		3 spring onions, trimmed and chopped	sprigs of fresh basil
		2 red peppers, deseeded and chopped	
		3 garlic cloves, chopped	fresh crusty rolls, to serve
15 minutes + 2–3 hours to chill		1 cucumber, peeled and chopped	
		1 tbsp red wine vinegar	
		1 tbsp chopped mixed herbs	
—		salt and pepper	

First, skin the tomatoes. Bring a kettle of water to the boil, put the tomatoes into a heatproof bowl, then pour over enough boiling water to cover them. Let them soak for about 3 minutes, then lift them out of the water and leave to cool slightly. When the tomatoes are cool enough to handle, gently pierce the skins with the point of a knife. Remove and discard the skins.

Halve the tomatoes and remove the seeds. Chop the flesh and put it into a food processor. Add the oil, spring onions, red peppers, garlic, cucumber, vinegar and mixed herbs to the food processor. Season with salt and pepper and blend until smooth. Strain the blended mixture through a sieve into a large bowl, then cover with clingfilm and refrigerate for 2–3 hours.

Ladle the chilled soup into serving bowls and garnish with croûtons and sprigs of fresh basil. Serve with fresh crusty rolls.

vichyssoise

very easy	
serves 4	
15–20 minutes + 2¼ hours to cool/chill	
35 minutes	

ingredients

2 tbsp butter
2 shallots, chopped
2 large leeks, trimmed and sliced
450 g/1 lb potatoes, peeled and diced
1 tbsp chopped fresh chives
1 bay leaf
600 ml/1 pint vegetable stock
salt and pepper
125 ml/4 fl oz single cream

GARNISH
swirl of single cream
chopped fresh chives

fresh crusty rolls, to serve

Melt the butter in a large saucepan over a medium heat. Add the shallots and cook, stirring, for 2 minutes, until slightly softened. Add the leeks and cook, stirring, for a further 2 minutes. Add the potatoes, chives, bay leaf and stock and season with salt and pepper. Bring to the boil, then reduce the heat, cover the pan and simmer for 30 minutes. Remove from the heat and leave the soup to cool for 15 minutes.

Remove and discard the bay leaf, then transfer the soup into a food processor and blend until smooth (you may need to do this in batches). Transfer into a large bowl and stir in the cream. Cover with clingfilm and chill in the refrigerator for at least 2 hours.

When ready to serve, remove from the refrigerator and ladle into serving bowls. Garnish each bowl with a swirl of cream and some chopped fresh chives and serve with fresh crusty rolls.

leek & potato soup

very easy	
serves 4	
15–20 minutes + 10 minutes to cool	
35 minutes	

ingredients

2 tbsp butter
2 garlic cloves, chopped
3 large leeks, trimmed and sliced
450 g/1 lb potatoes, peeled and
    chopped into bite-sized chunks
1 tbsp chopped fresh parsley
1 tbsp chopped fresh oregano
1 bay leaf
850 ml/1½ pints vegetable stock

salt and pepper
200 ml/7 fl oz crème fraîche
100 g/3½ oz smoked firm cheese, such
    as Applewood, grated

GARNISH
chopped fresh parsley
fresh chives

thick slices of fresh crusty bread,
    to serve

Melt the butter in a large saucepan over a medium heat. Add the garlic and cook, stirring, for 1 minute. Add the leeks and cook, stirring, for a further 2 minutes. Add the potatoes, herbs and stock, and season with salt and pepper. Bring to the boil, then reduce the heat, cover the pan and simmer for 25 minutes. Remove from the heat, leave to cool for 10 minutes, then remove and discard the bay leaf.

Transfer half of the soup into a food processor and blend until smooth (you may need to do this in batches). Return to the saucepan with the rest of the soup, stir in the crème fraîche and reheat gently. Season with salt and pepper.

Remove from the heat and stir in the cheese. Ladle into serving bowls and garnish with chopped fresh parsley and chives. Serve with slices of fresh crusty bread.

pea & mint soup

		ingredients	
very easy		1 tbsp butter	sprigs of fresh mint, to garnish
		3 shallots, chopped	slices of fresh wholemeal bread,
serves 4		2 leeks, trimmed and finely chopped	to serve
		1 potato, peeled and chopped	
		450 g/1 lb frozen peas	
15 minutes + 10 minutes to cool		2 tbsp chopped fresh mint	
		850 ml/1½ pints vegetable stock	
		salt and pepper	
40 minutes			

Melt the butter in a large saucepan over a medium heat. Add the shallots and cook, stirring, for 2 minutes. Add the leeks and cook, stirring, for a further 2 minutes. Add the potato, peas, chopped mint and stock, and season with salt and pepper. Bring to the boil, then reduce the heat, cover the pan and simmer for 30 minutes. Remove the soup from the heat and leave to cool for 10 minutes.

Transfer the soup into a food processor and blend until smooth (you may need to do this in batches). Return to the saucepan, season with salt and pepper and reheat gently.

Remove from the heat and pour into serving bowls. Garnish with sprigs of fresh mint and serve with slices of fresh wholemeal bread.

creamy carrot & parsnip soup

		ingredients	
very easy	4 tbsp butter	GARNISH
	1 large onion, chopped	single cream
serves 4	450 g/1 lb carrots, peeled and chopped	sprigs of fresh coriander
	2 large parsnips, peeled and chopped	
	1 tbsp grated fresh root ginger	fresh crusty rolls, to serve
15–20 minutes + 10 minutes to cool	1 tsp grated orange rind	
	600 ml/1 pint vegetable stock	
	125 ml/4 fl oz single cream	
	salt and pepper	
55 minutes– 1 hour		

Melt the butter in a large saucepan over a low heat. Add the onion and cook, stirring, for 3 minutes, until slightly softened. Add the carrots and parsnips, cover the pan and cook, stirring occasionally, for about 15 minutes, until the vegetables have softened a little. Stir in the ginger, orange rind and stock. Bring to the boil, then reduce the heat, cover the pan and simmer for 30–35 minutes until the vegetables are tender. Remove from the heat and leave to cool for 10 minutes.

Transfer the soup into a food processor and blend until smooth (you may need to do this in batches). Return the soup to the saucepan, stir in the cream and season well with salt and pepper. Warm through gently over a low heat.

Remove from the heat and ladle into soup bowls. Garnish each bowl with a swirl of cream and a sprig of fresh coriander and serve the soup with fresh crusty rolls.

mushroom & sherry soup

		ingredients	
very easy		4 tbsp butter	3 tbsp plain flour
		2 garlic cloves, chopped	125 ml/4 fl oz milk
serves 4		3 onions, sliced	2 tbsp sherry
		450 g/1 lb mixed white and chestnut	125 ml/4 fl oz soured cream
		mushrooms, sliced	
		100 g/3½ oz fresh ceps or porcini	GARNISH
15 minutes		mushrooms, sliced	soured cream
		3 tbsp chopped fresh parsley	chopped fresh parsley
		500 ml/18 fl oz vegetable stock	
40 minutes		salt and pepper	fresh crusty rolls, to serve

Melt the butter in a large saucepan over a low heat. Add the garlic and onions and cook, stirring, for 3 minutes, until slightly softened. Add the mushrooms and cook for a further 5 minutes, stirring. Add the chopped parsley, pour in the stock and season with salt and pepper. Bring to the boil, then reduce the heat, cover the pan and simmer for 20 minutes.

Put the flour into a bowl, mix in enough milk to make a smooth paste, then stir it into the soup. Cook, stirring, for 5 minutes. Stir in the remaining milk and the sherry and cook for a further 5 minutes. Remove from the heat and stir in the soured cream. Return the pan to the heat and warm gently.

Remove from the heat and ladle into serving bowls. Garnish with soured cream and chopped fresh parsley, and serve with fresh crusty rolls.

vegetable soup with pesto

		ingredients	
very easy		2 tbsp olive oil	1 tbsp chopped fresh basil
		2 garlic cloves, chopped	
serves 4		2 onions, chopped	PESTO
		1 celery stick, trimmed and chopped	2 garlic cloves, chopped
		1 carrot, peeled and chopped	25 g/1 oz fresh basil leaves
		1.2 litres/2 pints vegetable stock	85 g/3 oz Parmesan cheese, grated
20 minutes		1 potato, peeled and chopped	5 tbsp extra-virgin olive oil
		175 g/6 oz frozen peas	100 g/3½ oz pine kernels
		400 g/14 oz canned cannellini	sprigs of fresh basil, to garnish
45 minutes		beans, drained	
		salt and pepper	fresh focaccia, to serve

Heat 2 tablespoons of olive oil a large saucepan over a low heat.
Add the garlic and onions and cook, stirring, for 3 minutes, until
slightly softened. Add the celery and carrot and cook for a further
5 minutes, stirring. Pour in the stock, then add the potato, peas
and beans. Season with salt and pepper. Bring to the boil, then
reduce the heat, cover the pan and simmer for 30 minutes.

Meanwhile, to make the pesto, put all the ingredients into a food
processor and blend until smooth.

Stir the chopped basil into the soup and cook for a further
5 minutes. Remove from the heat and ladle into serving bowls.
Garnish each bowl with a generous tablespoonful of pesto and
a sprig of basil and serve with fresh focaccia.

asparagus & lemon soup

		ingredients	
 very easy		2 tbsp butter	salt and pepper
		3 leeks, trimmed and sliced	450 g/1 lb young, tender asparagus,
serves 4		1 celery stick, trimmed and sliced	cut into 2.5-cm/1-inch pieces
		1.2 litres/2 pints vegetable stock	125 ml/4 fl oz single cream
15–20 minutes + 10 minutes to cool		1 tbsp finely grated lemon rind	fine strips of lemon peel, to garnish
		2 tbsp lemon juice	
		1 potato, peeled and chopped	fresh crusty rolls, to serve
40 minutes		1 tbsp chopped fresh parsley	

Melt the butter in a large saucepan over a medium heat. Add the leeks and cook, stirring, for 3 minutes, until slightly softened. Add the celery and cook for a further 3 minutes, stirring. Add the stock, lemon rind and juice, potato and parsley, and season with salt and pepper. Bring to the boil, then reduce the heat, cover the pan and simmer for 25 minutes. Add the asparagus and cook for a further 5 minutes. Remove from the heat and leave to cool for 10 minutes.

Transfer half of the soup into a food processor and blend until smooth. Return to the pan with the rest of the soup, stir in the cream and reheat gently.

Remove from the heat and ladle into serving bowls. Garnish with fine strips of lemon peel and serve with fresh crusty rolls.

onion soup with croûtons

very easy	
serves 4	
15–20 minutes	
1 hour	

ingredients

100 g/3½ oz butter
2 garlic cloves, crushed
3 large onions, thinly sliced
1 tsp sugar
2 tbsp plain flour
225 ml/8 fl oz dry white wine
1.5 litres/2¾ pints vegetable stock
salt and pepper

CROUTONS
2 tbsp olive oil
2 slices day-old white bread,
    crusts removed

thick slices of fresh wholemeal and
    white bread, to serve

Melt the butter in a large saucepan over a medium heat. Add the garlic, onions and sugar and cook, stirring, for about 25 minutes, until the onions have caramelised.

In a bowl, mix the flour with enough wine to make a smooth paste, then stir it into the onion mixture. Cook for 2 minutes, then stir in the remaining wine and the stock. Season with salt and pepper. Bring to the boil, then reduce the heat, cover the pan and simmer for 30 minutes.

Meanwhile, to make the croûtons, heat the oil in a frying pan until hot. Cut the bread into small cubes and cook over a high heat, stirring, for about 2 minutes, until crisp and golden. Remove from the heat, drain the croûtons on kitchen paper and reserve.

When the soup is cooked, remove from the heat and ladle into serving bowls. Scatter over some fried croûtons and serve with slices of wholemeal and white bread.

italian tomato soup

		ingredients	
very easy		2 tbsp extra-virgin olive oil	4 tbsp chopped fresh basil
		2 large garlic cloves, crushed	4 tbsp mascarpone
serves 4		1 large onion, chopped	
		900 g/2 lb ripe vine tomatoes, skinned	sprigs of fresh basil, to garnish
		(see page 8), deseeded and roughly	
		chopped, juices reserved	TO SERVE
20 minutes + 10 minutes to cool		425 ml/15 fl oz vegetable stock	small slices of fresh ciabatta
		salt and pepper	thinly sliced mozzarella
50–55 minutes			

Heat the oil in a large saucepan over a medium heat. Add the garlic and onion and cook, stirring, for about 2 minutes, until slightly softened. Add the tomatoes and their juices and cook for a further 3 minutes, then pour in the stock and season with salt and pepper. Bring to the boil, then lower the heat, cover the pan and simmer for about 35–40 minutes. Remove from the heat and leave to cool for 10 minutes.

Transfer half of the soup into a food processor and blend until smooth. Return to the pan with the rest of the soup, stir in the chopped basil and cook for a further 5 minutes. Stir in the mascarpone and heat through briefly.

Remove from the heat and ladle into serving bowls. Garnish with sprigs of fresh basil and serve with slices of ciabatta topped with thin slices of mozzarella.

sweet potato & stilton soup

		ingredients	
very easy		4 tbsp butter	pepper
		1 large onion, chopped	150 ml/5 fl oz double cream
serves 4		2 leeks, trimmed and sliced	150 g/5½ oz Stilton cheese, crumbled
		175 g/6 oz sweet potatoes, peeled and diced	2 tbsp finely crumbled Stilton cheese, to garnish
15–20 minutes + 10 minutes to cool		850 ml/1½ pints vegetable stock	
		1 tbsp chopped fresh parsley	slices of fresh bread, to serve
		1 bay leaf	
45 minutes			

Melt the butter in a large saucepan over a medium heat. Add the onion and leeks and cook, stirring, for about 3 minutes, until slightly softened. Add the sweet potatoes and cook for a further 5 minutes, stirring, then pour in the stock, add the parsley and bay leaf and season with pepper. Bring to the boil, then lower the heat, cover the pan and simmer for about 30 minutes. Remove from the heat and leave to cool for 10 minutes. Remove the bay leaf.

Transfer half of the soup into a food processor and blend until smooth. Return to the pan with the rest of the soup, stir in the cream and cook for a further 5 minutes. Gradually stir in the crumbled Stilton until melted (do not let the soup boil).

Remove from the heat and ladle into serving bowls. Garnish with finely crumbled Stilton and serve with slices of fresh bread.

seafood soups

Fish and shellfish are very nutritious and quick to cook. Many are low in calories and fat, yet rich in protein and nutrients such as B vitamins. They are also an excellent source of iodine, which helps to maintain a healthy thyroid gland and keeps the metabolism running efficiently. Above all, however, fish and shellfish are delicious, and impart a wonderful richness to soups. Always buy the freshest you can find, and you will be rewarded with soups that are unparalleled in terms of quality and flavour.

traditional salmon soup

		ingredients	
very easy	2 tbsp butter	salt and pepper
	1 onion, chopped	300 g/10½ oz skinless salmon fillets,
serves 4	1 leek, trimmed and sliced	cut into bite-sized pieces
	1 tbsp plain flour	2 egg yolks
	700 ml/1¼ pints fish stock	100 ml/3½ fl oz double cream
15 minutes	1 large potato, peeled and chopped	
	1 tbsp chopped fresh parsley	sprigs of fresh dill, to garnish
	1 tbsp chopped fresh dill	
40 minutes		slices of crusty bread, to serve

Melt the butter in a large pan over a medium heat. Add the onion and leek and cook, stirring, for 3 minutes, until slightly softened. In a bowl, mix the flour with enough stock to make a smooth paste and stir it into the pan. Cook, stirring, for 1 minute, then gradually stir in the remaining stock with the potato, parsley and dill. Season with salt and pepper. Bring to the boil, then lower the heat, cover the pan and simmer for 25 minutes.

Add the salmon to the pan and cook for about 6 minutes until cooked through. In a clean bowl, whisk together the egg yolks and cream, then stir into the soup.

Remove from the heat and ladle into serving bowls. Garnish with sprigs of fresh dill and serve with slices of crusty bread.

tuna chowder

	ingredients	
very easy	2 tbsp butter	salt and pepper
	1 large garlic clove, chopped	1 courgette, trimmed and chopped
	1 large onion, sliced	225 g/8 oz canned tuna in
serves 4	1 carrot, peeled and chopped	brine, drained
	600 ml/1 pint fish stock	1 tbsp chopped fresh basil
	400 g/14 oz potatoes, peeled and cut	1 tbsp chopped fresh parsley
15–20 minutes	into bite-sized chunks	100 ml/3½ fl oz double cream
	400 g/14 oz canned chopped tomatoes	
	400 g/14 oz canned cannellini	sprigs of fresh basil, to garnish
50 minutes	beans, drained	thick slices of wholemeal bread,
	1 tbsp tomato purée	to serve

Melt the butter in a large saucepan over a low heat. Add the garlic and onion and cook, stirring, for 3 minutes, until slightly softened. Add the carrot and cook for a further 5 minutes, stirring. Pour in the stock, then add the potatoes, tomatoes, beans and tomato purée. Season with salt and pepper. Bring to the boil, then reduce the heat, cover the pan and simmer for 20 minutes.

Add the courgette, tuna, and chopped basil and parsley and cook for a further 15 minutes. Stir in the cream and cook very gently for a further 2 minutes.

Remove from the heat and ladle into individual serving bowls. Garnish with sprigs of fresh basil, and serve with thick slices of fresh wholemeal bread.

cullen skink

		ingredients		
very easy	2 tbsp butter	450 g/1 lb potatoes, peeled, cooked
	1 onion, chopped	and mashed
serves 4	1 leek, trimmed and chopped	6 tbsp double cream
	2 tbsp plain flour	
	850 ml/1½ pints milk	chopped fresh parsley, to garnish
15 minutes	1 bay leaf	TO SERVE
	2 tbsp chopped fresh parsley	fresh crusty rolls
	salt and pepper	fresh green salad
40 minutes	350 g/12 oz smoked haddock	
	fillets, skinned	

Melt the butter in a large saucepan over a medium heat. Add the onion and leek and cook, stirring, for about 3 minutes, until slightly softened. In a bowl, mix the flour with enough milk to make a smooth paste, then stir it into the pan. Cook, stirring, for 2 minutes, then gradually stir in the remaining milk. Add the bay leaf and chopped parsley and season. Bring to the boil, then lower the heat and simmer for 15 minutes.

Rinse the haddock fillets under cold running water, drain, cut into bite-sized chunks and add them to the soup. Cook for 15 minutes, until the fish is tender and cooked right through. Add the mashed potatoes and stir in the cream. Cook for a further 2–3 minutes, then remove from the heat and discard the bay leaf.

Ladle into serving bowls, garnish with chopped fresh parsley and serve with fresh crusty rolls and a fresh green salad.

haddock & prawn chowder

		ingredients	
very easy		1 tbsp butter	125 g/4½ oz frozen sweetcorn,
		1 onion, chopped	defrosted
serves 4		3 tbsp plain flour	250 g/9 oz prawns, cooked and peeled
		500 ml/18 fl oz fish stock	200 ml/7 fl oz double cream
		1 bay leaf	
		salt and pepper	whole cooked prawns, to garnish
20 minutes		500 ml/18 fl oz milk	TO SERVE
		2 tbsp dry white wine	fresh wholemeal bread
		juice and grated rind of 1 lemon	fresh green salad
40 minutes		450 g/1 lb haddock fillets, skinned	

Melt the butter in a large saucepan over a medium heat. Add the onion and cook, stirring, for about 3 minutes, until slightly softened. In a bowl, mix the flour with enough stock to make a smooth paste and stir it into the pan. Cook, stirring, for 2 minutes, then gradually stir in the remaining stock. Add the bay leaf and season with salt and pepper. Bring to the boil, then lower the heat. Pour in the milk and wine, and stir in the lemon juice and grated rind. Simmer for 15 minutes.

Rinse the haddock under cold running water, then drain and cut into bite-sized chunks. Add them to the soup with the sweetcorn. Cook for 15 minutes, until the fish is tender and cooked through. Stir in the prawns and the cream. Cook for a further 2–3 minutes, then remove from the heat and discard the bay leaf.

Ladle into serving bowls, garnish with whole cooked prawns and serve with fresh wholemeal bread and a fresh green salad.

mixed fish soup

		ingredients	
	very easy	1 tbsp butter	300 g/10½ oz cod fillets, skinned
		2 shallots, chopped	200 g/7 oz canned or freshly
		1 leek, trimmed and sliced	cooked crabmeat
	serves 4	3 tbsp plain flour	150 g/5½ oz canned sweetcorn,
		500 ml/18 fl oz fish stock	drained
		1 bay leaf	200 ml/7 fl oz double cream
	20 minutes	salt and pepper	
		500 ml/18 fl oz milk	TO GARNISH
		2 tbsp dry sherry	sprigs of fresh dill
		2 tbsp lemon juice	wedges of lemon
	40 minutes	300 g/10½ oz haddock fillets, skinned	fresh crusty rolls, to serve

Melt the butter in a large saucepan over a medium heat. Add the shallots and leek and cook, stirring, for about 3 minutes, until slightly softened. In a bowl, mix the flour with enough stock to make a smooth paste, then stir it into the pan. Cook, stirring, for 2 minutes, then gradually stir in the remaining stock. Add the bay leaf and season with salt and pepper. Bring to the boil, then lower the heat. Pour in the milk and sherry, and stir in the lemon juice. Simmer for 15 minutes.

Rinse the haddock and cod fillets under cold running water, then drain and cut into bite-sized chunks. Add to the soup with the crabmeat and sweetcorn. Cook for 15 minutes, until the fish is tender and cooked through. Stir in the cream. Cook for another 2–3 minutes, then remove from the heat and discard the bay leaf.

Ladle into serving bowls, garnish with sprigs of fresh dill and lemon wedges and serve with fresh crusty rolls.

bouillabaisse

	ingredients	
easy	100 ml/3½ fl oz olive oil	200 g/7 oz live mussels
	3 garlic cloves, chopped	250 g/9 oz snapper or monkfish fillets
serves 4	2 onions, chopped	250 g/9 oz haddock fillets, skinned
	2 tomatoes, deseeded and chopped	200 g/7 oz prawns, peeled and
	700 ml/1¼ pints fish stock	deveined
20 minutes +10 minutes to soak	400 ml/14 fl oz white wine	100 g/3½ oz scallops
	1 bay leaf	salt and pepper
	pinch of saffron threads	
	2 tbsp chopped fresh basil	fresh baguettes, to serve
45 minutes	2 tbsp chopped fresh parsley	

Heat the oil in a large pan over a medium heat. Add the garlic and
onions and cook, stirring, for 3 minutes. Stir in the tomatoes,
stock, wine, bay leaf, saffron and herbs. Bring to the boil, reduce
the heat, cover and simmer for 30 minutes. Meanwhile, soak the
mussels in lightly salted water for 10 minutes. Scrub the shells
under cold running water and pull off any beards. Discard any with
broken shells. Tap the remaining mussels and discard any that
refuse to close. Put the rest into a large pan with a little water,
bring to the boil and cook over a high heat for 4 minutes. Remove
from the heat and discard any that remain closed.

When the tomato mixture is cooked, rinse the fish, pat dry and cut
into chunks. Add to the pan and simmer for 5 minutes. Add the
mussels, prawns and scallops and season. Cook for 3 minutes, until
the fish is cooked through. Remove from the heat, discard the bay
leaf and ladle into serving bowls. Serve with fresh baguettes.

seafood soup

	ingredients	
easy	1 kg/2 lb 4 oz live mussels	300 ml/10 fl oz double cream
	150 ml/5 fl oz dry white wine	1 tbsp cornflour
serves 4	2 tbsp butter	200 g/7 oz prawns, peeled
	1 onion, sliced	and deveined
	1 leek, trimmed and sliced	100 g/3½ oz scallops
15 minutes + 10 minutes to soak	850 ml/1½ pints water	salt and pepper
	pinch of saffron threads	
	250 g/9 oz snapper fillets, skinned	sprigs of fresh dill, to garnish
35 minutes	250 g/9 oz haddock fillets, skinned	fresh wholemeal rolls, to serve

Soak the mussels in salted water for 10 minutes. Scrub under cold running water; pull off any beards. Discard any with broken shells and any that refuse to close when tapped. Put the rest into a pan with the wine; bring to the boil. Cook over a high heat for 4 minutes. Discard any that remain closed. Leave to cool. Lift out the mussels; remove the shells. Strain the cooking liquid and reserve. Melt the butter in a pan over a medium heat. Add the onion and leek. Cook, stirring, for 3 minutes. Stir in the water, saffron and cooking liquid. Bring to the boil, lower the heat and simmer for 15 minutes.

Rinse the fish fillets, pat dry and cut into small chunks. Add to the pan and simmer for 5 minutes. Stir in the cream. Blend the cornflour in 2 tablespoons of water and stir into the soup. Add the prawns and scallops, season and cook for 2 minutes. Add the mussels and cook for 1 minute. Remove from the heat and ladle into serving bowls. Garnish with dill and serve with fresh rolls.

crab & vegetable soup

	ingredients	
very easy	2 tbsp chilli oil	1 tbsp grated lime rind
	1 garlic clove, chopped	6 kaffir lime leaves, finely shredded
serves 4	4 spring onions, trimmed and sliced	300 g/10½ oz freshly cooked crabmeat
	2 red peppers, deseeded and chopped	200 g/7 oz freshly cooked crab claws
	1 tbsp grated fresh root ginger	150 g/5½ oz canned sweetcorn,
15–20 minutes	1 litre/1¾ pints fish stock	drained
	salt and pepper	2 tbsp chopped fresh coriander
	100 ml/3½ fl oz coconut milk	
40 minutes	100 ml/3½ fl oz rice wine or sherry	TO GARNISH
	2 tbsp lime juice	chopped fresh coriander
		thin strips of lime peel

Heat the oil in a large saucepan over a medium heat. Add the garlic and spring onions and cook, stirring, for about 3 minutes, until slightly softened. Add the red peppers and ginger and cook for a further 4 minutes, stirring. Pour in the stock and season with salt and pepper. Bring to the boil, then lower the heat. Pour in the coconut milk, rice wine and lime juice, and stir in the grated lime rind and kaffir lime leaves. Simmer for 15 minutes.

Add the crabmeat and crab claws to the soup with the sweetcorn and coriander. Cook the soup for 15 minutes, until the fish is tender and cooked right through.

Remove from the heat and ladle into serving bowls. Garnish with chopped fresh coriander and strips of lime peel and serve.

spicy wonton soup

		ingredients	
easy		2 garlic cloves, chopped	SOUP
		2 spring onions, trimmed and chopped	1 tbsp chilli oil or sesame oil
		2 tsp light soy sauce	3 spring onions, trimmed and sliced
serves 4		2 tsp sherry	1 small red chilli, deseeded and finely
		2 tbsp chopped fresh coriander	chopped
		2 egg whites	1 red pepper, deseeded and chopped
20 minutes		100 g/3½ oz cooked prawns, peeled	1 litre/1¾ pints fish stock
		and chopped	1 tbsp light soy sauce
		100 g/3½ oz cooked chicken	2 tbsp sherry
25 minutes		meat, chopped	1 tbsp chopped fresh coriander
		16 wonton wrappers	1 tbsp chopped fresh parsley

To make the wontons, put the garlic, spring onions, soy sauce, sherry, coriander and 1 egg white into a large bowl and mix well. Divide the mixture between 2 smaller bowls, then add the prawns to one bowl and the chicken to the other. Spoon some prawn mixture into the centres of 8 wonton wrappers, brush round the edges with the remaining egg white, then fold over into triangles and seal well. Take the 2 furthest corners of each triangle and join with egg white. Repeat the process with the remaining 8 wonton wrappers, this time using the chicken mixture.

To make the soup, heat the oil in a large frying pan over a medium heat. Add the spring onions. Cook, stirring, for 3 minutes. Add the chilli and pepper. Cook, stirring, for 5 minutes. Pour in the stock, soy sauce, sherry and herbs. Bring to the boil, lower the heat and simmer for 10 minutes. Add the wontons. Cook for 5–6 minutes. Remove from the heat, ladle into serving bowls and serve hot.

prawn & vegetable bisque

very easy	
serves 4	
15 minutes + 10 minutes to cool	
35 minutes	

ingredients

3 tbsp butter
1 garlic clove, chopped
1 onion, sliced
1 carrot, peeled and chopped
1 celery stick, trimmed and sliced
1.2 litres/2 pints fish stock
4 tbsp red wine
1 tbsp tomato purée
1 bay leaf

salt and pepper
600 g/1 lb 5 oz prawns, peeled and deveined
100 ml/3½ fl oz double cream

GARNISH
swirls of single cream
whole cooked prawns

Melt the butter in a large saucepan over a medium heat. Add the garlic and onion and cook, stirring, for 3 minutes, until slightly softened. Add the carrot and celery and cook for a further 3 minutes, stirring. Pour in the stock and red wine, then add the tomato purée and bay leaf. Season with salt and pepper. Bring to the boil, then lower the heat and simmer for 20 minutes. Remove from the heat and leave to cool for 10 minutes, then remove and discard the bay leaf.

Transfer half of the soup into a food processor and blend until smooth (you may need to do this in batches). Return to the pan with the rest of the soup. Add the prawns and cook over a low heat for 5–6 minutes.

Stir in the cream and cook for a further 2 minutes, then remove from the heat and ladle into serving bowls. Garnish with swirls of single cream and whole cooked prawns and serve at once.

poultry & meat soups

The recipes in this section draw on a wide variety of ingredients and dishes from around the world, such as Scotch Broth and Indian Mulligatawny. There is also a continental-style Salami & Vegetable Chowder, and a Pork & Vegetable Broth bursting with delicious Thai flavours. And for the cost-conscious among you, the Turkey & Lentil Soup provides an excellent way of using leftover turkey at Christmas or at other times during the year. You can also substitute leftover chicken for the turkey whenever the need arises.

chicken & potato soup
with bacon

		ingredients	
very easy	1 tbsp butter	200 g/7 oz skinless chicken
	2 garlic cloves, chopped	breast, chopped
serves 4	1 onion, sliced	salt and pepper
	250 g/9 oz smoked lean back bacon,	4 tbsp double cream
	chopped	
	2 large leeks, trimmed and sliced	grilled bacon, chopped, to garnish
15 minutes	2 tbsp plain flour	fresh crusty rolls, to serve
	1 litre/1¾ pints chicken stock	
40 minutes	800 g/1 lb 12 oz potatoes, peeled	
	and chopped	

Melt the butter in a large saucepan over a medium heat. Add the garlic and onion and cook, stirring, for 3 minutes, until slightly softened. Add the chopped bacon and leeks and cook for a further 3 minutes, stirring. In a bowl, mix the flour with enough stock to make a smooth paste, then stir it into the pan. Cook, stirring, for 2 minutes. Pour in the remaining stock, then add the potatoes and chicken. Season with salt and pepper. Bring to the boil, then lower the heat and simmer for 25 minutes, until the chicken and potatoes are tender and cooked through.

Stir in the cream and cook for a further 2 minutes, then remove from the heat and ladle into serving bowls. Garnish with chopped bacon and serve with fresh crusty rolls.

cream of chicken soup

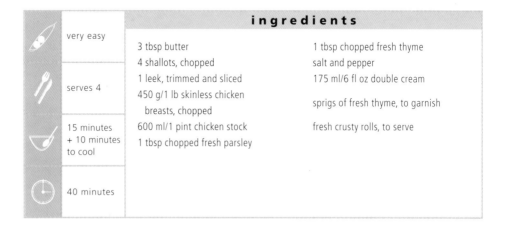

very easy	
serves 4	
15 minutes + 10 minutes to cool	
40 minutes	

ingredients

3 tbsp butter
4 shallots, chopped
1 leek, trimmed and sliced
450 g/1 lb skinless chicken
  breasts, chopped
600 ml/1 pint chicken stock
1 tbsp chopped fresh parsley

1 tbsp chopped fresh thyme
salt and pepper
175 ml/6 fl oz double cream

sprigs of fresh thyme, to garnish

fresh crusty rolls, to serve

Melt the butter in a large saucepan over a medium heat. Add the shallots and cook, stirring, for 3 minutes, until slightly softened. Add the leek and cook for a further 5 minutes, stirring. Add the chicken, stock and herbs, and season with salt and pepper. Bring to the boil, then lower the heat and simmer for 25 minutes, until the chicken is tender and cooked through. Remove from the heat and leave to cool for 10 minutes.

Transfer the soup into a food processor and blend until smooth (you may need to do this in batches). Return the soup to the pan and warm over a low heat for 5 minutes.

Stir in the cream and cook for a further 2 minutes, then remove from the heat and ladle into serving bowls. Garnish with sprigs of thyme and serve with fresh crusty rolls.

turkey & lentil soup

		ingredients	
very easy		1 tbsp olive oil	1 carrot, peeled and chopped
		1 garlic clove, chopped	200 g/7 oz red lentils
serves 4		1 large onion, chopped	salt and pepper
		200 g/7 oz mushrooms, sliced	350 g/12 oz cooked turkey
		1 red pepper, deseeded and chopped	meat, chopped
		6 tomatoes, skinned (see page 8),	1 courgette, trimmed and chopped
20 minutes		deseeded and chopped	1 tbsp shredded fresh basil
		1.2 litre/2 pints chicken stock	
		150 ml/5 fl oz red wine	basil leaves, to garnish
50 minutes		85 g/3 oz cauliflower florets	thick slices of fresh crusty bread,
			to serve

Heat the oil in a large saucepan. Add the garlic and onion and cook over a medium heat, stirring, for 3 minutes, until slightly softened. Add the mushrooms, red pepper and tomatoes and cook for a further 5 minutes, stirring. Pour in the stock and red wine, then add the cauliflower, carrot and red lentils. Season with salt and pepper. Bring to the boil, then lower the heat and simmer the soup gently for 25 minutes, until the vegetables are tender and cooked through.

Add the turkey and courgette to the pan and cook for 10 minutes. Stir in the shredded basil and cook for a further 5 minutes, then remove from the heat and ladle into serving bowls. Garnish with basil leaves and serve with fresh crusty bread.

indian mulligatawny

		ingredients	
very easy		2 tbsp vegetable oil	150 g/5½ oz potatoes, peeled
		1 garlic clove, chopped	and chopped
serves 4		1 large onion, chopped	1 tbsp curry powder
		150 g/5½ oz mushrooms, sliced	salt and pepper
		2 tbsp plain flour	1 tbsp chopped fresh coriander
15–20 minutes		1 litre/1¾ pints chicken stock	125 ml/4 fl oz double cream
		200 g/7 oz skinless chicken	
		breasts, chopped	GARNISH
		150 g/5½ oz lean smoked	grated fresh coconut
45 minutes		ham, chopped	sprigs of fresh coriander
		1 carrot, peeled and chopped	fresh naan bread, to serve

Heat the oil in a large saucepan. Add the garlic and onion and cook over a medium heat, stirring, for 3 minutes, until slightly softened. Add the mushrooms and cook for a further 2 minutes. In a bowl, mix the flour with enough stock to make a smooth paste, then stir it into the pan. Stir in the remaining stock, then add the chicken, ham, carrot, potatoes and curry powder and season with salt and pepper. Bring to the boil, then lower the heat and simmer for 30 minutes until the meat and vegetables are tender and cooked through.

Stir in the coriander and cream and cook for a further 5 minutes. Remove from the heat and ladle into serving bowls. Garnish with grated coconut and sprigs of coriander and serve with naan bread.

salami & vegetable chowder

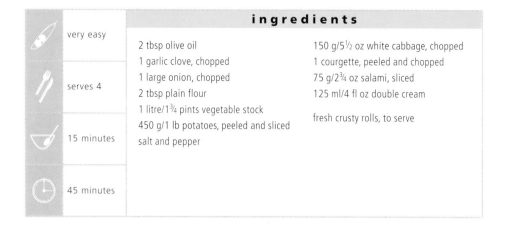

very easy	
serves 4	
15 minutes	
45 minutes	

ingredients

2 tbsp olive oil
1 garlic clove, chopped
1 large onion, chopped
2 tbsp plain flour
1 litre/1¾ pints vegetable stock
450 g/1 lb potatoes, peeled and sliced
salt and pepper

150 g/5½ oz white cabbage, chopped
1 courgette, peeled and chopped
75 g/2¾ oz salami, sliced
125 ml/4 fl oz double cream

fresh crusty rolls, to serve

Heat the oil in a large saucepan. Add the garlic and onion and cook over a medium heat, stirring, for 3 minutes, until slightly softened. In a bowl, mix the flour with enough stock to make a smooth paste, then stir it into the pan. Stir in the remaining stock, then add the potatoes and season with salt and pepper. Bring to the boil, then lower the heat and simmer for 25 minutes, until the vegetables are tender and cooked through.

Add the cabbage, courgette and salami and cook for 10 minutes. Stir in the cream and cook for a further 5 minutes. Remove from the heat, ladle into serving bowls and serve with fresh crusty rolls.

beef & cauliflower soup

	ingredients	
very easy	2 tbsp chilli oil	salt and pepper
	1 garlic clove, chopped	250 g/9 oz lean beef, sliced
	3 spring onions, trimmed and sliced	150 g/5½ oz cauliflower florets
serves 4	1 small red chilli, deseeded and	125 g/4½ oz broccoli florets
	finely chopped	
	1 red pepper, deseeded and chopped	TO SERVE
15–20	1 litre/1¾ pints beef stock	fresh green salad
minutes	1 tbsp soy sauce	fresh baguette
	2 tbsp rice wine or dry sherry	
	150 g/5½ oz potatoes, peeled	
40 minutes	and chopped	

Heat the oil in a large saucepan. Add the garlic, spring onions and chilli and cook over a medium heat, stirring, for 3 minutes, until slightly softened. Add the red pepper and cook for 5 minutes, stirring. Pour in the stock, soy sauce and rice wine, then add the potatoes and season with salt and pepper. Bring to the boil, then lower the heat and simmer for 15 minutes.

Add the beef, cauliflower and broccoli and cook for a further 15 minutes. Remove from the heat and ladle into serving bowls. Serve with a fresh green salad and fresh baguette.

cheese & bacon soup

very easy	
serves 4	
15 minutes	
40 minutes	

ingredients

2 tbsp butter
2 garlic cloves, chopped
1 large onion, sliced
250 g/9 oz smoked lean back
  bacon, chopped
2 large leeks, trimmed and sliced
2 tbsp plain flour
1 litre/1¾ pints vegetable stock
450 g/1 lb potatoes, peeled
  and chopped

salt and pepper
100 ml/3½ fl oz double cream
300 g/10½ oz Cheddar cheese, grated

grated Cheddar cheese, to garnish

fresh garlic bread, to serve

Melt the butter in a large saucepan over a medium heat. Add the garlic and onion and cook, stirring, for 3 minutes, until slightly softened. Add the chopped bacon and leeks and cook for a further 3 minutes, stirring. In a bowl, mix the flour with enough stock to make a smooth paste, then stir it into the pan. Cook, stirring, for 2 minutes. Pour in the remaining stock, then add the potatoes. Season with salt and pepper. Bring the soup to the boil, then lower the heat and simmer gently for 25 minutes, until the potatoes are tender and cooked through.

Stir in the cream and cook for 5 minutes, then gradually stir in the cheese until melted. Remove from the heat and ladle into serving bowls. Garnish with grated Cheddar cheese and serve with fresh garlic bread.

pork & vegetable broth

		ingredients	
very easy		1 tbsp chilli oil	1 small red chilli, deseeded and
		1 garlic clove, chopped	finely chopped
		3 spring onions, trimmed and sliced	1 tbsp grated fresh root ginger
serves 4		1 red pepper, deseeded and	salt and pepper
		finely sliced	115 g/4 oz fine egg noodles
		2 tbsp cornflour	200 g/7 oz canned water chestnuts,
15 minutes		1 litre/1¾ pints vegetable stock	drained and sliced
		1 tbsp soy sauce	
		2 tbsp rice wine or dry sherry	TO SERVE
45 minutes		150 g/5½ oz pork fillet, sliced	fresh green salad
		1 tbsp finely grated lemon grass	fresh crusty bread

Heat the oil in a large saucepan. Add the garlic and spring onions and cook over a medium heat, stirring, for 3 minutes, until slightly softened. Add the red pepper and cook for a further 5 minutes, stirring. In a bowl, mix the cornflour with enough of the stock to make a smooth paste, then stir it into the pan. Cook, stirring, for 2 minutes. Stir in the remaining stock and the soy sauce and rice wine, then add the pork, lemon grass, chilli and ginger. Season with salt and pepper. Bring to the boil, then lower the heat and simmer for 25 minutes.

Bring a separate saucepan of water to the boil, add the noodles and cook for 3 minutes. Remove from the heat, drain, then add the noodles to the soup along with the water chestnuts. Cook for a further 2 minutes, then remove from the heat and ladle into serving bowls. Serve with a fresh green salad and crusty bread.

sausage & red cabbage soup

very easy	
serves 4	
15 minutes	
50 minutes	

ingredients

2 tbsp olive oil
1 garlic clove, chopped
1 large onion, chopped
1 large leek, trimmed and sliced
2 tbsp cornflour
1 litre/1¾ pints vegetable stock
450 g/1 lb potatoes, peeled and sliced
200 g/7 oz skinless sausages, sliced

salt and pepper
150 g/5½ oz red cabbage, chopped
200 g/7 oz canned black-eyed
  beans, drained
125 ml/4 fl oz double cream

ground paprika, to garnish

fresh crusty rolls, to serve

Heat the oil in a large saucepan. Add the garlic and onion and cook over a medium heat, stirring, for 3 minutes, until slightly softened. Add the leek and cook for a further 3 minutes, stirring. In a bowl, mix the cornflour with enough stock to make a smooth paste, then stir it into the pan. Cook, stirring, for 2 minutes. Stir in the remaining stock, then add the potatoes and sausages. Season with salt and pepper. Bring to the boil, then lower the heat and simmer for 25 minutes.

Add the red cabbage and beans and cook for 10 minutes, then stir in the cream and cook for a further 5 minutes. Remove from the heat and ladle into serving bowls. Garnish with ground paprika and serve with fresh crusty rolls.

scotch broth

		ingredients	
very easy		75 g/2¾ oz pearl barley, rinsed and drained	250 g/9 oz potatoes, peeled and sliced
			1 large carrot, peeled and chopped
serves 4		1 tbsp vegetable oil	150 g/5½ oz swede, peeled and chopped
		1 garlic clove, chopped	
		1 large onion, chopped	1 turnip, peeled and chopped
		1 large leek, trimmed and sliced	2 celery sticks, trimmed and sliced
20 minutes		1.2 litre/2 pints vegetable stock	2 tsp dried mixed herbs
		1 bay leaf	sprigs of fresh parsley, to garnish
		450 g/1 lb lean boneless lamb, fat trimmed away	thick slices of fresh wholemeal bread, to serve
1½ hours		salt and pepper	

Bring a saucepan of water to the boil. Add the barley and boil over a high heat for 5 minutes, skimming the surface when necessary. Remove from the heat and reserve.

Heat the oil in a large saucepan. Add the garlic and onion and cook over a medium heat, stirring, for 3 minutes, until slightly softened. Add the leek and cook for a further 4 minutes, stirring. Stir in the stock, then drain the barley and add to the pan along with the bay leaf. Cut the lamb into bite-sized chunks and add to the pan. Season with salt and pepper. Bring to the boil, then lower the heat and simmer for 15 minutes. Add the potatoes, carrot, swede, turnip, celery and mixed herbs and cook for 1 hour.

Remove from the heat, discard the bay leaf and ladle into serving bowls. Garnish the Scotch broth with sprigs of fresh parsley and serve with slices of fresh wholemeal bread.

beans, grains & noodles

Comforting soups containing beans, grains and noodles are heartwarming at any time of the year. Many of the recipes in this section use canned beans because they are convenient, but you can use dried if you prefer. Simply adjust the soaking and cooking times accordingly. The times vary according to the type of bean, so always check the instructions on the packet. Whether you use canned or dried beans, these soups are highly nutritious, and many need only fresh crusty bread to transform them into satisfying meals in themselves.

spicy lentil soup

		ingredients	
very easy		1 tbsp olive oil	1 tbsp chopped fresh parsley
		1 onion, sliced	pinch of saffron threads
serves 4		1 leek, trimmed and sliced	1 tsp ground coriander
		1.3 litres/2¼ pints vegetable stock	1 tsp garam masala
		1 carrot, peeled and chopped	salt and pepper
10–15 minutes		1 celery stick, trimmed and sliced	
		75 g/2¾ oz brown rice	sprigs of fresh coriander, to garnish
		250 g/7 oz red lentils	fresh wholemeal bread, to serve
50 minutes		1 bay leaf	

Heat the oil in a large saucepan. Add the onion and cook over a
medium heat, stirring, for 3 minutes, until slightly softened. Add
the leek and cook for a further 2 minutes, stirring. Stir in the stock,
then add the carrot, celery, rice, lentils, herbs and spices. Season
with salt and pepper. Bring to the boil, then lower the heat and
simmer for 40 minutes until the rice, lentils and vegetables are
tender and cooked through.

Remove the soup from the heat and discard the bay leaf. Ladle
into serving bowls, garnish with sprigs of fresh coriander and serve
with fresh wholemeal bread.

pea & ham soup

		ingredients	
	very easy	1 tbsp butter	1 tbsp chopped fresh tarragon
		1 onion, sliced	salt and pepper
	serves 4	1 leek, trimmed and sliced	4 tbsp double cream
		1 litre/1¾ pints vegetable stock	
		450 g/1 lb freshly shelled peas, or	GARNISH
	10–15 minutes + 10 minutes to cool	frozen peas, defrosted	cooked ham, chopped
		200 g/7 oz lean smoked ham, chopped	sprigs of fresh tarragon
		1 bay leaf	fresh crusty rolls, to serve
	45 minutes		

Melt the butter in a large saucepan over a medium heat. Add the onion and cook, stirring, for 3 minutes, until slightly softened. Add the leek and cook for a further 2 minutes, stirring. Stir in the stock, then add the peas, ham, bay leaf and tarragon. Season with salt and pepper. Bring to the boil, then lower the heat and simmer for 30 minutes. Remove from the heat and discard the bay leaf. Leave to cool for 10 minutes.

Transfer half of the soup into a food processor and blend until smooth. Return to the pan with the rest of the soup, stir in the cream and cook over a low heat for a further 5 minutes.

Remove the soup from the heat and ladle into serving bowls. Garnish with chopped ham and sprigs of fresh tarragon and serve with fresh crusty rolls.

soupe au pistou

		ingredients
very easy		

PISTOU SAUCE | 450g/1 lb potatoes, chopped
50 g/1¾ oz fresh basil, chopped | 1 large carrot, peeled and chopped
25 g/1 oz fresh parsley, chopped | 100 g/3½ oz thin French beans
3 garlic cloves, finely chopped | 200 g/7 oz canned cannellini beans
5 tbsp extra-virgin olive oil | 150g/5½ oz smoked ham, chopped
3 tbsp freshly grated Parmesan | 400 g/14 oz canned tomatoes
FOR THE SOUP | 1 tbsp chopped fresh thyme
2 tbsp extra-virgin olive oil | salt and pepper
1 garlic clove, finely chopped | 75 g/2¾ oz dried vermicelli
1 onion, chopped | shavings of fresh Parmesan, to garnish
1.2 litres/2 pints vegetable stock | thick slices of fresh bread, to serve

very easy

serves 4

25 minutes

35 minutes

To make the pistou, put all the ingredients into a food processor and process until blended. Transfer into a bowl, cover with clingfilm and chill until required.

To make the soup, heat the oil in a large saucepan over a medium heat, add the garlic and the onion and cook, stirring, for 3 minutes, until slightly softened. Stir in the stock, then add the potatoes, carrot, French beans (that have been topped and tailed, then finely chopped), drained cannellini beans, ham, and the tomatoes with their juices. Stir in the thyme and season. Bring to the boil, then lower the heat and simmer for 20 minutes. Add the vermicelli and cook for a further 12 minutes, or according to the instructions on the packet.

Remove from the heat and ladle into serving bowls. Put a generous spoonful of pistou sauce into each bowl, garnish with fresh Parmesan shavings and serve with thick slices of fresh bread.

mixed bean soup with gruyère

	ingredients	
very easy	1 tbsp extra-virgin olive oil	1 tbsp chopped fresh thyme
	3 garlic cloves, finely chopped	1 tbsp chopped fresh oregano
	4 spring onions, trimmed and sliced	salt and pepper
serves 4	200 g/7 oz mushrooms, sliced	175 g/6 oz Gruyère cheese, grated
	1 litre/1¾ pints vegetable stock	4 tbsp double cream
15 minutes	1 large carrot, peeled and chopped	
+ 10 minutes	400 g/14 oz canned mixed	GARNISH
to cool	beans, drained	swirls of single cream
	800 g/1 lb 12 oz canned	finely chopped spring onions
55 minutes	chopped tomatoes	thick slices of fresh bread, to serve

Heat the oil in a large saucepan over a medium heat. Add the garlic and spring onions and cook, stirring, for 3 minutes, until slightly softened. Add the mushrooms and cook for a further 2 minutes, stirring. Stir in the stock, then add the carrot, mixed beans, chopped tomatoes and herbs. Season with salt and pepper. Bring to the boil, then lower the heat and simmer for 30 minutes. Remove from the heat and leave to cool for 10 minutes.

Transfer into a food processor and blend until smooth. Return to the pan and stir in the cheese. Cook for a further 10 minutes, then stir in the cream. Cook for 5 minutes, then remove from the heat and ladle into serving bowls. Garnish with swirls of cream and chopped or sliced spring onions. Serve with slices of fresh bread.

sweet potato & lentil soup

		ingredients	
	very easy	1 tbsp olive oil	1 carrot, peeled and chopped
		1 garlic clove, chopped	200 g/7 oz red lentils
	serves 4	1 large onion, chopped	salt and pepper
		1 red pepper, deseeded and chopped	1 tbsp chopped fresh basil
	15–20 minutes + 10 minutes to cool	6 tomatoes, skinned (see page 8), deseeded and chopped	sprigs of fresh basil, to garnish
		1 litre/1¾ pints vegetable stock	fresh crusty rolls, to serve
	55 minutes	450 g/1 lb sweet potatoes, peeled and chopped	

Heat the oil in a large saucepan. Add the garlic and onion and cook over a medium heat, stirring, for 3 minutes, until slightly softened. Add the red pepper and the tomatoes and cook for a further 2 minutes, stirring. Pour in the stock, then add the sweet potatoes, carrot and lentils. Season with salt and pepper. Bring to the boil, then lower the heat and simmer for 30 minutes, until all of the vegetables are tender and cooked through. Remove from the heat and leave to cool for 10 minutes.

Transfer half of the soup into a food processor and blend until smooth. Return to the pan with the rest of the soup and cook for 10 minutes. Stir in the chopped basil and cook for a further 5 minutes. Remove from the heat and ladle into serving bowls. Garnish with sprigs of fresh basil and serve with fresh crusty rolls.

chorizo & red kidney bean soup

		ingredients

very easy	2 tbsp olive oil
	2 garlic cloves, chopped
	2 red onions, chopped
	1 red pepper, deseeded and chopped
	2 tbsp cornflour
	1 litre/1¾ pints vegetable stock
	450 g/1 lb potatoes, peeled, halved
	  and sliced
		salt and pepper
		150 g/5½ oz chorizo, sliced
		2 courgettes, trimmed and sliced
		200 g/7 oz canned red kidney
		  beans, drained
		125 ml/4 fl oz double cream
		
		thick slices of fresh bread, to serve

serves 4		
15–20 minutes		
50 minutes		

Heat the oil in a large saucepan. Add the garlic and onions and cook over a medium heat, stirring, for 3 minutes, until slightly softened. Add the red pepper and cook for a further 3 minutes, stirring. In a bowl, mix the cornflour with enough stock to make a smooth paste and stir it into the pan. Cook, stirring, for 2 minutes. Stir in the remaining stock, then add the potatoes and season with salt and pepper. Bring to the boil, then lower the heat and simmer for 25 minutes, until the vegetables are tender.

Add the chorizo, courgettes and kidney beans to the pan. Cook for 10 minutes, then stir in the cream and cook for a further 5 minutes. Remove from the heat and ladle into serving bowls. Serve with slices of fresh bread.

tomato, rice & tarragon soup

		ingredients	
very easy	2 tbsp olive oil	175 g/6 oz brown rice
	2 garlic cloves, chopped	1 tbsp chopped fresh tarragon
serves 4	2 red onions, chopped	salt and pepper
	1 red pepper, deseeded and chopped	100 ml/3 ½ fl oz double cream
	8 tomatoes, skinned (see page 8), deseeded and chopped	sprigs of fresh tarragon, to garnish
20 minutes + 10 minutes to cool	1 litre/1¾ pints vegetable stock	fresh crusty bread, to serve
	1 celery stick, trimmed and sliced	
50 minutes		

Heat the oil in a large saucepan. Add the garlic and onions and cook over a medium heat, stirring, for 3 minutes, until slightly softened. Add the red pepper and the tomatoes and cook for a further 2 minutes, stirring. Stir in the stock, then add the celery, rice and tarragon. Season with salt and pepper. Bring to the boil, then lower the heat and simmer for 30 minutes. Remove from the heat and leave to cool for 10 minutes.

Transfer half of the soup into a food processor and blend until smooth. Return to the pan with the rest of the soup and cook for 5 minutes. Stir in the cream and cook for a further 5 minutes. Remove from the heat and ladle into serving bowls. Garnish with sprigs of fresh tarragon and serve with fresh crusty bread.

chicken, mushroom & barley soup

very easy	
serves 4	
15 minutes	
1 ½ hours	

ingredients

75 g/2¾ oz pearl barley, rinsed and drained

2 tbsp butter

1 large onion, sliced

1 large leek, trimmed and sliced

1 litre/1¾ pints chicken stock

salt and pepper

450 g/1 lb skinless chicken breasts, chopped

250 g/9 oz chestnut mushrooms, sliced

1 large carrot, peeled and chopped

1 tbsp chopped fresh oregano

1 bay leaf

sprigs of fresh flat-leaved parsley, to garnish

fresh crusty bread, to serve

Bring a saucepan of water to the boil. Add the barley and boil over a high heat for 5 minutes, skimming the surface when necessary. Remove from the heat and reserve.

Melt the butter in a large saucepan. Add the onion and cook over a medium heat, stirring, for 3 minutes, until slightly softened. Add the leek and cook for a further 4 minutes, stirring. Stir in the stock, then drain the barley and add to the pan. Season with salt and pepper. Bring to the boil, then lower the heat and simmer for 45 minutes. Add the chicken, mushrooms, carrot, oregano and bay leaf. Cook for a further 30 minutes.

Remove from the heat and discard the bay leaf. Ladle into serving bowls, garnish with sprigs of fresh flat-leaved parsley and serve with fresh crusty bread.

minestrone

		ingredients	
very easy		2 tbsp olive oil	100 g/3½ oz green leafy
		2 garlic cloves, chopped	cabbage, shredded
serves 4		2 red onions, chopped	75 g/2¾ oz frozen peas, defrosted
		75 g/2¾ oz Parma ham, sliced	1 tbsp chopped fresh parsley
		1 red pepper, deseeded and chopped	salt and pepper
15–20 minutes		1 orange pepper, deseeded and chopped	75 g/2¾ oz dried vermicelli
		400 g/14 oz canned chopped tomatoes	freshly grated Parmesan cheese, to garnish
		1 litre/1¾ pints vegetable stock	
45–50 minutes		1 celery stick, trimmed and sliced	fresh crusty bread, to serve
		400 g/14 oz canned borlotti beans	

Heat the oil in a large saucepan. Add the garlic, onions and Parma ham and cook over a medium heat, stirring, for 3 minutes, until slightly softened. Add the red and orange peppers and the chopped tomatoes and cook for a further 2 minutes, stirring. Stir in the stock, then add the celery. Drain and add the borlotti beans along with the cabbage, peas and parsley. Season with salt and pepper. Bring to the boil, then lower the heat and simmer for 30 minutes.

Add the vermicelli to the pan. Cook for a further 10–12 minutes, or according to the instructions on the packet. Remove from the heat and ladle into serving bowls. Garnish with freshly grated Parmesan and serve with fresh crusty bread.

tofu & noodle broth

very easy	
serves 4	
15 minutes	
5 minutes	

ingredients

1 tbsp sesame oil
1 garlic clove, chopped
4 spring onions, trimmed and sliced
1 small red chilli, deseeded and
  finely chopped
50 g/1¾ oz shiitake mushrooms, sliced
50 g/1¾ oz chestnut mushrooms,
  sliced
1 tbsp rice wine
2 tsp soy sauce

2 tbsp chopped fresh coriander
1 litre/1¾ pints vegetable stock
75 g/2¾ oz dried fine egg noodles
100 g/3½ oz firm tofu, drained and cut
  into small cubes
salt and pepper

chopped fresh coriander, to garnish

fresh crusty bread, to serve

Heat the oil in a large wok or saucepan over a high heat. Add the garlic, spring onions and chilli and stir-fry for 1 minute, until slightly softened. Add the mushrooms, rice wine, soy sauce, coriander and stock and bring to the boil. Lower the heat, add the noodles and simmer for 3 minutes.

Add the tofu and season with salt and pepper. Remove from the heat, then transfer into individual serving bowls. Garnish with chopped fresh coriander and serve with fresh crusty bread.

index